30°E  60°  90°  120°  150°

*Arctic Ocean*

*A S I A*

*EUROPE*

*AFRICA*

*A*

*Pacific*

*Ocean*

*Indian*

*Ocean*

*AUSTRALIA*

*ANTARCTICA*

# *Portugal*

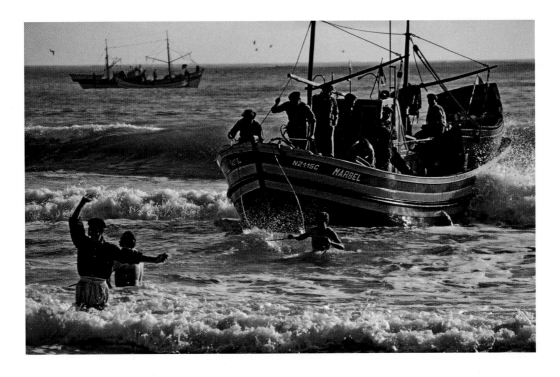

## Zilah Deckker

Timothy J. Coates and Ana Francisca de Azevedo, Consultants

**NATIONAL GEOGRAPHIC**
WASHINGTON, D.C.

# Contents

Portugal is a country of remarkable physical and cultural contrasts where Atlantic and Mediterranean influences come together. As the westernmost point of Europe, it is an unavoidable starting point for the exploration of modern European environmental and cultural history. The country occupies almost the whole western corner of the Iberian Peninsula. Its continental territory is shaped as a rough rectangle stretching north to south; the south of the country is strongly influenced by its Muslim heritage.

Portugal's heavily indented south and west coasts have many memorable beaches. In the west, strong winds attract surfers and other sportspeople, while the coast is still home to an ancient network of harbors and hardy fishing communities. In the south, beaches of white sand have calm, clear waters for scuba diving. Portugal's island groups, Madeira and the Azores, are natural wildlife sanctuaries where Atlantic and tropical influences meet.

Portugal has other unique qualities. It was largely rural until the late 1960s, and UNESCO lists rural and mountain regions as World Heritage sites, along with several historic Portuguese cities and villages.

Surrounded by myth and memory, the Portuguese landscape traces the rise and fall of ancient civilizations that occupied the region. Archaeological evidence from the Paleolithic period occurs everywhere, from rock engravings—the most extensive in Europe—to megalithic temples. Signs of Roman, Phoenician, and Carthaginian control are spread all over the country. Islamic Moorish occupation left its imprint on the south. Medieval architecture still forms the heart of the main cities. The landscape has been shaped by treaties and battles, and by new

arrivals who settled and put down roots throughout what became one of Europe's earliest nations. Opening an era of globalization, Portuguese explorers pioneered the modern age through their exploration and the "discovery" of the New World. Their contribution to the intellectual revolution of the 15th and 16th centuries was almost unparalleled.

The attraction of Portugal lies in its complex cosmopolitanism, its monuments, squares, and *bairros*, its popular and religious festivities and rituals, and its friendly people. This book is a good introduction to Portugal; it's up to you to come discover it all!

▲ **Workers remove tree bark from boiling water as part of the cork-making process. Portugal is the world's leading supplier of cork.**

Ana Francisca de Azevedo
Department of Geography
University of Minho, Portugal

# The Edge of Europe

PORTUGAL WAS ONCE DESCRIBED as the land "where the Earth ends and the sea begins." This was because Portugal is located on the western edge of the European continent, and any lands to the west across the Atlantic Ocean were unknown until the 15th century. Portugal has the most southwesterly point in Europe—Cabo de São Vicente, otherwise known as Cape St. Vincent. The cape is a rugged cliff that towers 246 feet (75 m) above the rough Atlantic waters.

Portugal itself occupies the southwest of the Iberian Peninsula. The country makes up one-fifth of the peninsula; the rest belongs to Spain. Despite being a small corner of Europe, Portugal has a rich landscape with a beach-lined coast, mountains, and fertile plains.

◀ The Ponta da Piedade area on the south coast of Portugal is dotted with rock formations that have been carved in the sandstone cliffs by the waves.

# WHAT'S THE WEATHER LIKE?

Portugal has a warm, maritime climate—its weather is governed by the ocean. The north is colder and wetter than the south. Summers are hot and dry throughout the country. The sea breeze keeps the coasts cool at the height of summer, but the temperatures of sheltered areas inland, such as the Alentejo, can soar to 104° F (40° C). In winter, it snows in the mountains in the north, while on the southern coast, the Algarve region enjoys pleasantly warm temperatures all year round. Rainfall is highest in the north, with the heaviest rain falling on the Serra da Estrela. The lowest rainfall is in the Algarve region.

## Fast Facts

**OFFICIAL NAME:** Portuguese Republic
**FORM OF GOVERNMENT:** Parliamentary democracy
**CAPITAL:** Lisbon
**POPULATION:** 10,676,910
**OFFICIAL LANGUAGE:** Portuguese
**MONETARY UNIT:** Euro
**AREA:** 35,655 square miles (92,391 square km)
**BORDERING NATION:** Spain
**HIGHEST POINTS:** Alto da Torre 6,532 feet (1,993 meters; mainland), Ponta do Pico 7,713 feet (2,351 meters; Azores islands)
**LOWEST POINT:** Atlantic Ocean 0 feet (0 meters)
**MAJOR MOUNTAIN RANGES:** Serra do Gerês, Serra da Estrela
**MAJOR RIVERS:** Tejo, Douro, Mondego, Minho

## Average Temperature & Rainfall

Average High/Low Temperatures; Yearly Rainfall
**PORTO (NORTH):** 66° F (19° C) / 50° F (10° C); 50 in (127 cm)
**LISBON (WEST):** 69° F (21° C) / 55° F (13° C); 29 in (74 cm)
**FARO (SOUTH):** 71° F (22° C) / 54° F (12° C); 21 in (53 cm)
**PONTO DELGADA (AZORES):** 68° F (20° C) / 57° F (14° C); 40 in (102 cm)

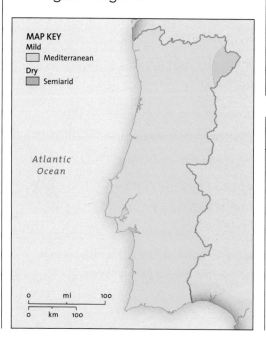

MAP KEY
Mild
◻ Mediterranean
Dry
◻ Semiarid

Atlantic Ocean

0        mi        100
0        km        100

Minho

Lima

*Serra do Gerês*

MOUNTAINS
AND LAKE,
page 11

● Bragança

● Braga

*Tras-os-Montes*

Vila Real ●

STEEL ROAD
BRIDGE,
page 12

Porto (Oporto) ●

*Douro*

Aveiro ●

Viseu ●

*Mondego*

● Guarda

BEIRA
INTERIOR

*Serra da Estrela*

+ Torre
(Highest point on
Mainland Portugal)
6,539 ft
1,993 m

Coimbra ●

*Beira Litoral*

# PORTUGAL

Leiria ●

Castelo
Branco ●

FLOCK OF SHEEP
ON HILLSIDE,
page 13

*Barragem
de Pracana*

*Rio Tejo (Tagus)*

Portalegre ●

## Atlantic
## Ocean

Santarém ●

*Barragem
de Montargil*

*Barragem
do Maranhão*

SPAIN

Amadora ●

Lisboa
(Lisbon) ⊛

FLOWERS
IN MEADOW,
page 14

*A L E N T E J O*

Sintra ●

Palmela ●

Évora ●

*Barragem
de Alqueva*

Setúbal ●

*Guadiana*

### Azores

Corvo

Flores

Graciosa
São Jorge
Faial

Terceira

Horta ●
Pico

+ Ponta do Pico
7,713 ft
2,351 m

SNOW-CAPPED
VOLCANO,
page 12

São
Miguel

Santa Maria

*Atlantic
Ocean*

Sines ●

Beja ●

## MAP KEY

⊛ National capital

● Selected city

+ Elevation

0    miles    50

0    km    50

0   mi   100
0   km   100

### Madeira Islands

*Atlantic Ocean*

Porto
Santo

*Madeira*

CLIFF FORMATIONS
AND BEACH,
pages 2, 6-7

*A L G A R V E*

Faro ●

HOTELS AND
TOURIST BEACH,
page 15

● Funchal

*Ilhas
Desertas*

POINTED
MOUNTAIN,
page 11

0   mi   20
0   km   20

*Cabo
de São
Vicente*

*Ponta da
Piedade*

*Ria
Formosa*

RIVERS AND
ISLANDS,
page 15

LIGHTHOUSE,
page 10

### Globe inset
Europe
PORTUGAL
Atlantic
Ocean
Africa

### Azores / Madeira inset
*Atlantic
Ocean*

*Azores
inset*

PORTUGAL

SPAIN

*Madeira
Inset*

MOROCCO

## Physical Map

# Small but Strong

Portugal is a rough rectangle about 345 miles (550 km) long and 125 miles (200 km) wide. It is about the size of the U.S. state of Maine.

## GATEWAY TO THE WORLD

Rocky Cape St. Vincent has been seen as an important place for centuries. The ancient Greeks called it the Land of Serpents; the Romans knew it as the Holy Promontory. The cliff is named after a Spanish saint who was buried there in the 4th century A.D. In 1420, Prince Henry settled in Sagres, near the cape. Henry was interested in mapmaking and navigation. He paid for many of the early expeditions of the great Portuguese explorers.

▲ The lighthouse on Cape St. Vincent is built on the site of a 16th-century fortress.

Portugal is one of the oldest nations in the world. It became an independent kingdom in the 12th century A.D., and its present borders with Spain—its only neighbor—have not really changed since the 13th century. Apart from a period of about 60 years between 1580 and 1640, when the kingdom was united with Spain, Portugal has been a fiercely independent nation throughout its 800-year history and has developed a language and culture quite distinct from Spain's.

## Looking to the Sea

Because of Portugal's position on the southwest edge of Europe and its long Atlantic coastline, the Portuguese became pioneers of exploring the oceans. Among many famous Portuguese explorers was Ferdinand Magellan, who led the first voyage around the world between 1519 and 1522.

Other Portuguese expeditions discovered islands far out in the Atlantic. Two of these island groups—the Azores and Madeira—still belong to the country.

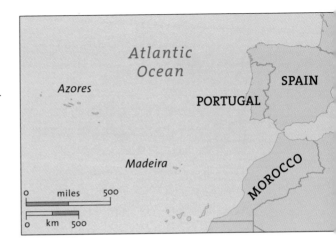

## Divided Land

The largest river in Portugal, the Tejo (Tagus in English), runs across the middle of the country. It divides Portugal into two major regions: the mountainous north and the rolling plains in the south.

The west of the country is covered by a coastal plain. Mountains and high hills spread south from the Cantabrian Mountains of Spain and cover the northeastern third of the country. The mountains slope down to rolling hills, giving way to the lowlands of the Alentejo in the center and then the coastal plains of the Algarve in the extreme south.

▲ The Azores are halfway between Portugal and Canada. The Madeira Islands are nearer to Morocco.

▼ Madeira Island is an enormous volcano that rises from the deep ocean floor. The island is dotted with ancient craters.

# ISOLATED ISLANDS

**N**early 1,000 miles (1,600 km) off the coast is Portugal's most distant territory—the Azores. These are nine main islands in three groups and many more unpopulated islets. The islands are part of the Mid-Atlantic Ridge, a range of mountains that runs along the ocean floor. Most of the peaks are underwater, but the Azores region is one of the few places where the range breaks the surface.

The Azores are volcanic islands. The last eruption was in the 1950s. Lake Furnas, on São Miguel Island, is heated by volcanic activity. Rocks on the lake's shoreline are hot enough to cook on! The islands also have frequent earthquakes.

▲ Pico Island is dominated by Ponto do Pico, a giant volcano, which is the tallest peak in Portugal.

▼ The Douro River reaches the ocean at Porto, where it is crossed by the Dom Luís I Bridge—a tall iron structure built in 1886.

Portugal is divided into seven geographical regions. These coincide with the country's historical provinces. In the north are the Minho-Douro Litoral and the Trás-os-Montes. The center is divided into the Beira Litoral, the Beira Interior, and Estremadura-Ribatejo. The south is made up of Alentejo and the Algarve.

# Mountain Time Capsule

Portugal's northern mountains belong to larger ranges that cross the border with Spain. The north was the place where the nation of Portugal began; the south was added a few hundred years later. The mountains are the least populated area in the country, dotted with ancient villages. The main cities are Porto and Coimbra.

The Minho-Douro region makes up the northwest and has granite hills covered with dense shrubs and woodlands. Only the very tops of the tallest peaks are bare rock. The Trás-os-Montes—meaning "behind the mountains"—in the northeast is a high plateau with rocky peaks and deep valleys. The plateau slopes down to the Douro River Valley, which is Portugal's main grape-growing region.

South of the Douro are the Beira regions: the name means "shores." The Beira Litoral, on the Atlantic coast, is a plain with pinewoods and sand dunes. The Beira Interior inland is the most mountainous of the Beira regions. Its main mountain range is the Serra da Estrela, home to the highest peak in mainland Portugal.

▲ A flock of sheep graze on the rocky mountains above the Beira Litoral lowlands.

▲ Wildflowers cover
a wide meadow in the
Alentejo region in spring.

# Big Rivers

Most of Portugal's rivers begin in the center of Spain and cross Portugal to reach the Atlantic. The two most important rivers are the Douro and the Tejo. Their valleys are fertile farming regions, and the rivers are traditionally important routes to the coast and the world beyond. The main port at the mouth of the Douro is Porto, while the nation's capital, Lisbon, is at the mouth of the Tejo in the Estremadura-Ribatejo region. The Tejo empties into a bay that provides Lisbon with an excellent natural harbor.

# Beyond the Tejo

Alentejo means "beyond the Tejo," and this area begins south of the Tejo River. It is a dry plain that covers a third of the country. This is the natural habitat of the cork oak—the most important agricultural product in the country—and the olive tree. The Alentejo is Portugal's main farming region.

## ISLANDS OF SAND

The eastern Algarve is home to remarkable sand islands. Little can grow there, so traditionally the islands are home to fishing communities. The region also has a long history of producing salt by evaporating sea water.

▶ The sand islands form at the mouth of the Ria Formosa.

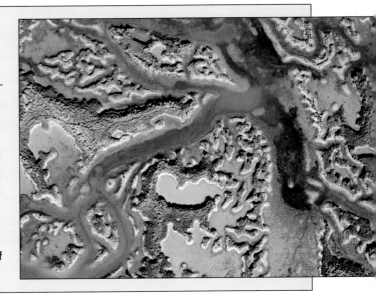

## *The South Coast*

With its long stretches of sandy beaches and warm climate, the Algarve has become a major vacation destination for both Portuguese and foreigners. The main city is Faro, which, along with other coastal towns, has expanded rapidly in the last few decades.

▼ The beaches along the western end of the Algarve coast are popular tourist resorts.

# A Country of Forests

THERE IS A SAYING IN PORTUGAL: "The eucalyptus are for us, the pines are for our children, and the cork is for our grandchildren." Eucalyptus trees grow fast and can be cut in a few years, the pines take 30 years to grow, and the cork oaks take several decades before they are ready to be harvested.

Forestry is important in Portugal. A quarter of the country is covered with forests. They are important as a source of lumber and other products, such as cork, and to protect the animals and other plants that live there. Tree roots also hold the soil together and protect dry land from erosion. In the north, much land is used to grow grape vines. Plantations of olive, fig, almond, and carob trees are common elsewhere.

◀ A forest of stone pines grows on sand dunes on the southern coast of Portugal. The pines are also known as umbrella trees because they provide a lot of shade.

# CHANGING NATURE

Portugal has been inhabited since the Stone Age—at least 10,000 years ago. In that time, humans have changed the natural landscape in many ways. In the Stone Age, most of Portugal would have been covered by forest. Today just a quarter of that area is still forested. In many ways the modern forests may look very similar to the ancient habitat, but over hundreds of generations, people have shaped the forests to meet their needs. Native species, such as robur, tauzin, holm, and cork oaks are still the most common trees. However, about a third of the plants are foreign species that have been introduced by people. One of the most widespread newcomers is the eucalyptus.

Changes to the forests occurred slowly, so Portugal's rural communities are well integrated with the natural world. Portugal has modernized at a slower rate than other parts of Europe. Even today there are many villages in which the way of life has remained the same for centuries.

▶ **A sperm whale calf follows its mother past the Azores. The Azores and Madeira islands are good places to see sperm whales and many other types of whales.**

## Species at Risk

A survey by the Portuguese Institute for the Conservation of Nature has shown that of 551 animal species studied, 297 were in danger of becoming rare or even going extinct. The report said that the main reason for these problems was the destruction of natural habitats. Such damaging activities have become much more widespread in the last 20 years since Portugal joined the European Union (EU). In that time money from the EU has been used to build roads, dams, and tourist resorts—at the expense of nature. However, 5 percent of the land is protected in some way, including one national park, eleven nature reserves, eight conservation areas, and many more protected landscapes.

Species at risk include:
> Black vulture
> Chamois (goat)
> Iberian barbel (fish)
> Iberian eagle
> Iberian lynx
> Madeiran land snail
> Monk seal

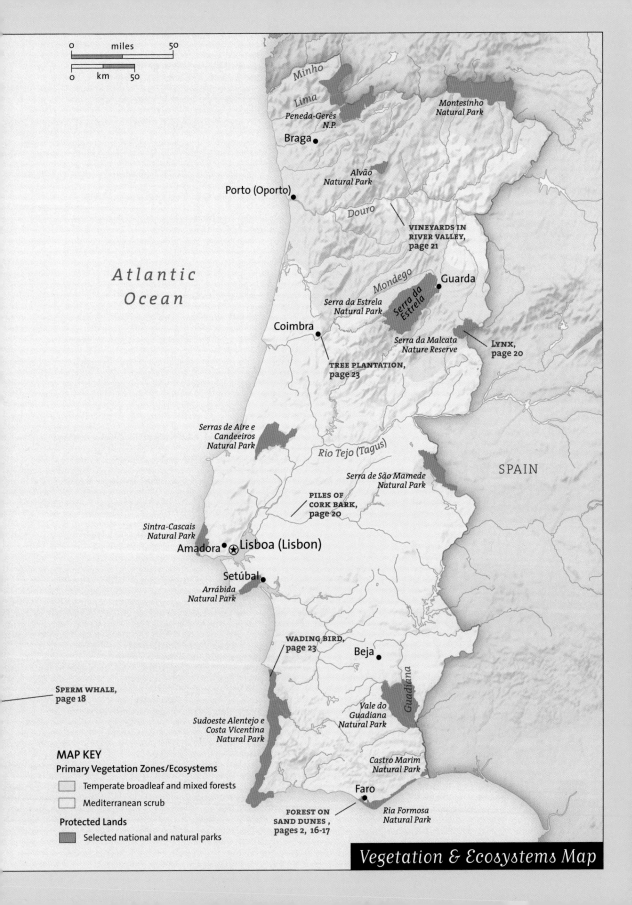

*Minho*

*Lima*

*Peneda-Gerês
N.P.*

*Montesinho
Natural Park*

Braga

*Alvão
Natural Park*

Porto (Oporto)

*Douro*

**VINEYARDS IN
RIVER VALLEY,
page 21**

*Atlantic
Ocean*

*Mondego*

Guarda

*Serra da Estrela
Natural Park*

*Serra da
Estrela*

*Serra da Malcata
Nature Reserve*

← **LYNX,
page 20**

**TREE PLANTATION,
page 23**

*Serras de Aire e
Candeeiros
Natural Park*

*Rio Tejo (Tagus)*

*Serra de São Mamede
Natural Park*

**SPAIN**

**PILES OF
CORK BARK,
page 20**

*Sintra-Cascais
Natural Park*

Amadora ● ⊛ Lisboa (Lisbon)

Setúbal

*Arrábida
Natural Park*

**WADING BIRD,
page 23**

Beja

*Guadiana*

**SPERM WHALE,
page 18**

*Sudoeste Alentejo e
Costa Vicentina
Natural Park*

*Vale do
Guadiana
Natural Park*

*Castro Marim
Natural Park*

## MAP KEY

### Primary Vegetation Zones/Ecosystems

Temperate broadleaf and mixed forests

Mediterranean scrub

### Protected Lands

Selected national and natural parks

**FOREST ON
SAND DUNES ,
pages 2, 16-17**

Faro

*Ria Formosa
Natural Park*

## Vegetation & Ecosystems Map

▲ A tall stack of cork bark is left to dry in the sun after being stripped from tree trunks.

## A Tree of Life

The cork oak tree is the unofficial national symbol of Portugal. Forests of cork oak are found in many parts of the country, but mostly in the Alentejo region. For generations the Portuguese have stripped the soft, spongy bark from the trunk of the tree. The stripped bark is known as cork and is used for many things from the stoppers in wine bottles to floats and even parts of airplanes. Harvesting cork is an important part of the Portuguese economy and way of life. The newly stripped trees are easy to spot in the landscape with their naked trunks shining yellow and reddish, while piles of fresh cork are left to dry in the hot sun.

## THE MISSING LYNX

The Iberian lynx (right) is the most endangered cat species in the world. Only a few hundred exist in the Reserva Natural da Serra da Malcata, which spreads across the Portugal-Spain border. The two nations are cooperating on a program to create corridors of forests through the mountains, so the cats can move around and find mates more easily.

▲ The hills above the
Douro River in northern
Portugal are covered in
grape vines used to
make the country's
famous wines.

A stripped cork oak tree renews its bark within nine years, when it can be harvested again. Cork is an environmentally-friendly product, as no damage is caused to the trees. The tree's acorns are also used to feed farm animals, such as pigs. Cattle feed on the grass beneath the cork trees. One-third of the world's cork oak trees grow in Portugal, and the country is the largest producer of cork products in the world.

## Changing Animals

Thousands of years of farming and hunting by humans has meant that few large animals are left living wild in Portugal. The common mammals are boars, wild goats, fallow deer, roe deer, foxes, and Iberian hares. Most wild hunting animals are very rare. The Iberian lynx is now almost extinct in Portugal. The wolf still survives in remote parts, such as the Serra da Estrela.

## A REMOTE CORNER

In 1971 Portugal's first national park, Peneda-Gerês, was set up in the mountains of the northwest. The park protects species such as wolves and polecats, which are rare in the rest of Europe. There are also 18 species of plants that grow nowhere else. The park is home to a breed of dogs called the *cão de castro laboreiro*, or the cattle dog. This smart breed is a favorite choice for use as the country's police dogs.

Humans have brought new species to the country, mostly from Africa. New arrivals include the chameleon and the mongoose.

## Sea Creatures

Portugal has 500 miles (800 km) of coast, and its people have always had a close relationship with the sea. For centuries, villages on the coast have survived by fishing. Crabs, clams, and oysters are collected from the seabed. Portuguese fishing boats hunt for huge schools of sardines and larger fish such as tuna, cod, and bonito.

## Flying Visitors

Bird life in Portugal is very rich because the country is an important stopover point for migratory species

▼ Tuna gather in large groups near the African and Portuguese coasts to feed on schools of sardines.

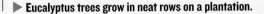

# FAST-GROWING FOREIGNERS

The eucalyptus tree was brought from Australia to Portugal in the middle of the 19th century. Its soft wood is good for making paper. Today eucalyptus trees have become an important forestry product, and plantations cover large areas. In recent years, however, environmentalists have warned that the eucalyptus is a destructive plant. The plantations suck water from the soil and do not support much wildlife.

▶ Eucalyptus trees grow in neat rows on a plantation.

coming to and from central Europe each year. These visitors include stilts, avocets, curlews, and black-tailed godwits, which migrate to West Africa for the winter. They rest in Portugal's wetlands before making the dangerous journey across the Sahara Desert. The Algarve is a great place for bird-watching, mainly in the coastal nature reserves of Ria Formosa, Castro Marim, and Cape St. Vincent.

## Foreign Plants

Portuguese explorers returned with unusual plants from distant lands. Many of these exotic species have become common in the forests. In the 17th century, monks planted Himalayan pines, Japanese camphor trees, and Lebanese cedars on the hills at Buçaco. Lisbon's Botanical Garden is one of the oldest in Europe, with a wide variety of tropical plants, some over 100 years old.

▼ A black-winged stilt's long legs allow the bird to wade through the shallow marshes along Portugal's coasts.

# Changing
## the
# World

**P**ORTUGAL'S HISTORY HAS BEEN DRIVEN BY its position sandwiched between Spain and the Atlantic Ocean. Traveling overland from Portugal required a journey through Spain, so the Portuguese looked for a new way to reach foreign lands—across the ocean. Portuguese ships were the first to make a proper exploration of the Atlantic Ocean. By the 15th century, they were sailing huge distances during what is known as the Age of Discovery. By the 1550s, Portuguese explorers had established trading posts and colonies in what are now Brazil, Japan, Africa, India, and China. This had an enormous impact on the world, as civilizations that had been isolated by the ocean were now able to trade with and learn from one another.

◀ Sagres, used as a training vessel by the Portuguese navy, leads a tall ship race out of Lisbon harbor in an echo of voyages during the Age of Discovery.

# ANCIENT CIVILIZATIONS

The earliest remains of human settlements in Portugal date back to 8000 B.C. The country has been populated by several waves of people over the years. The Phoenicians, originally from what is now Lebanon, came to the west coast in the 12th century B.C. Celts from central Europe arrived in the 8th century. They were followed by Greeks and later Carthaginians from North Africa. The Romans arrived in the 3rd century B.C. They knew the region as Lusitania, and it was the westernmost province of the Roman Empire for 700 years.

▼ Roman rule was the first time the land that is now Portugal was one region. This mosaic in Conimbriga is one of the largest to have survived since Roman times.

In A.D. 711, Moors—Muslim people from North Africa—settled in the southern Iberian Peninsula. Over several centuries, Christian armies slowly pushed the Moors out of Iberia. By the 9th century, northern Portugal was under Christian rule, and in 1143, Portugal emerged as a Christian kingdom separate from the rest of Iberia. It was ruled by a king until 1910 when the country became a republic.

## Time line

This chart shows some of the important dates in the history of Portugal from the departure of the Romans in the 5th century A.D to the present day.

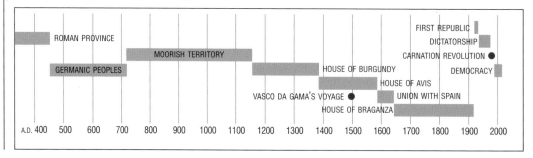

ROMAN PROVINCE
FIRST REPUBLIC
DICTATORSHIP
MOORISH TERRITORY
CARNATION REVOLUTION ●
GERMANIC PEOPLES
DEMOCRACY
HOUSE OF BURGUNDY
HOUSE OF AVIS
VASCO DA GAMA'S VOYAGE ●
UNION WITH SPAIN
HOUSE OF BRAGANZA

A.D. 400  500  600  700  800  900  1000  1100  1200  1300  1400  1500  1600  1700  1800  1900  2000

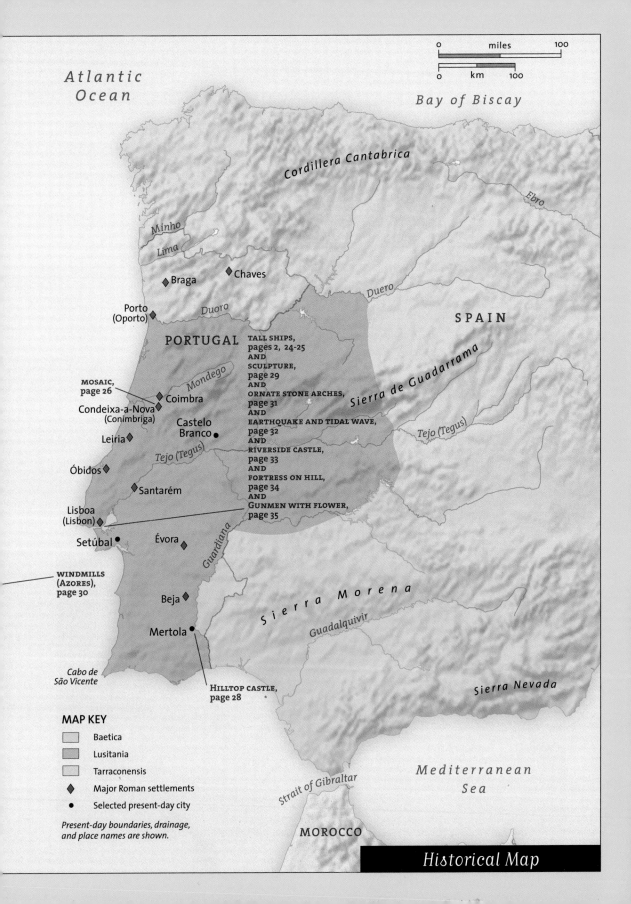

Atlantic
Ocean

Bay of Biscay

*Cordillera Cantabrica*

*Ebro*

*Minho*

*Lima*

◆ Braga     ◆ Chaves

*Duero*

Porto
(Oporto) ◆     *Duoro*

SPAIN

PORTUGAL     **TALL SHIPS,**
**pages 2, 24-25**
**AND**
**SCULPTURE,**
**page 29**
**AND**
**ORNATE STONE ARCHES,**
**page 31**
**AND**
**EARTHQUAKE AND TIDAL WAVE,**
**page 32**
**AND**
**RIVERSIDE CASTLE,**
**page 33**
**AND**
**FORTRESS ON HILL,**
**page 34**
**AND**
**GUNMEN WITH FLOWER,**
**page 35**

*Mondego*

**MOSAIC,**
**page 26**
◆ Coimbra

Condeixa-a-Nova
(Conimbriga) ◆

Castelo
Branco ●

Leiria ◆

*Tejo (Tegus)*

*Sierra de Guadarrama*

*Tejo (Tegus)*

Óbidos ◆

Santarém ◆

Lisboa
(Lisbon) ◆

Setúbal ●     Évora ◆

*Guardiana*

**WINDMILLS**
**(AZORES),**
**page 30**

Beja ◆

*Sierra    Morena*

Mertola ●

*Guadalquivir*

*Cabo de
São Vicente*

**HILLTOP CASTLE,**
**page 28**

*Sierra Nevada*

## MAP KEY

| | Baetica |
| | Lusitania |
| | Tarraconensis |
| ◆ | Major Roman settlements |
| ● | Selected present-day city |

*Present-day boundaries, drainage,
and place names are shown.*

*Strait of Gibraltar*

*Mediterranean
Sea*

**MOROCCO**

*Historical Map*

o ____ miles ____ 100

o ____ km ____ 100

# A Kingdom Found

The kingdom of Portugal was formed during the wars between the Moors and European armies, who wanted the whole of Iberia to be ruled by Christians. There were many battles between the 8th and 12th centuries as new leaders began holy wars, or crusades. One of the crusaders was Count Henry of Burgundy, who ruled part of what is now France. Henry had an older brother, and so would never be king of Burgundy. He was looking for

## VERY MOORISH

Moors from North Africa arrived in Spain in the 8th century A.D. and soon spread into what is now Portugal. They colonized the south of the country. The Moors spoke Arabic and they named the southern coast *al-Gharb*, which means "the west." The region is still known as the Algarve. The Moors remained until the 13th century. They introduced new sciences and mathematics and were the first to grow rice, oranges, and lemons in Portugal. Many cities still have Moorish features, and Portuguese has 600 words that come from Arabic.

▼ A Moorish castle still stands above the walled town of Mertola.

another territory to rule. Henry's army helped to push the Moors out of much of Iberia including what is now northern Portugal. As a reward for his success, King Afonso VI of Castile made him the Count of Portucale. (Castile was a kingdom covering most of Spain at the time.) Henry also married Afonso's daughter and had a son, Afonso Henriques. In 1147 Afonso Henriques captured Lisbon from the Moors and declared Portugal separate from the rest of Iberia.

He made himself King Afonso I. His successors expanded the territory and, in 1249, Afonso III conquered the last Moorish enclave in the Algarve and established the present borders of Portugal.

## Age of Empire

In 1383 Fernando I, the last king of the House of Burgundy, died without a son. To stop Portugal from becoming a Spanish province, Fernando's half brother, João I, became king—the first in the House of Avis.

One of João's sons is now remembered as Henry the Navigator. Henry brought together the finest seamen and mapmakers to explore the Atlantic Ocean. This was the start of the Age of Discovery that made Portugal the greatest sea power of the time.

▼ The Monument to the Discoveries in Lisbon shows Portugal's great explorers, such as Vasco da Gama and Pedro Álvares Cabral, who discovered Brazil. The figures are led by Henry the Navigator.

When Henry died in 1460, Portugal had explored the west coast of Africa and had discovered the Madeira, Azores, and Cape Verde islands. In 1498, Vasco da Gama found a way of reaching India by sea by sailing around the southern tip of Africa. In 1500 Pedro Álvares Cabral discovered Brazil.

## Building Success

Their new colonies and trade routes made the Portuguese royal family the richest in Europe. In the 16th century, Lisbon was the business capital of the world. Money was spent on beautiful churches and palaces built in an elaborate style of architecture called Manueline after Manuel I, the king at the time. The buildings were covered in symbols of seafaring such as ropes, knots, and globes.

Portugal was at the height of its power for only a short while. When Henry I, the Cardinal-King died in 1580, the Spanish invaded and annexed Portugal. Philip II of Spain was crowned

▼ Windmills were a major source of power in the Azores. They were built according to designs introduced by settlers from Belgium in the late 15th century.

Philip I of Portugal. Portugal remained under Spanish rule until 1640 when João IV was crowned king and began the House of Braganza.

## *Riches and Disaster*

By the time Portugal regained its independence, its empire had become less powerful. The Dutch had taken control of the Far East and Britain dominated India. Only Brazil remained entirely Portuguese, despite attacks from the Dutch and the French. In the late 17th century, gold was found in Brazil. Brazilian gold made the Portuguese royals fabulously wealthy, but the money was not used wisely. Ordinary Portuguese did not really benefit.

▲ The stone carvings around these windows at Jerónimos Monastery in Lisbon show the knotted rope style of Manueline architecture.

## THE QUARTER OF THE EXPLORERS

Belém is in western Lisbon. Vasco da Gama sailed from there on his voyage to India in 1498. The district is now known for the Jerónimos Monastery and the Tower of Belém, which were built in the early 16th century. Both are made from *pedra lioz*, a golden-colored limestone that is found nearby. When they were built, Portugal was at the height of its power and enjoyed fabulous wealth from trade with India and the Far East. The tower and monastery are now symbols of Portuguese power during the Age of Discovery. In 1960, the Monument to the Discoveries was built nearby.

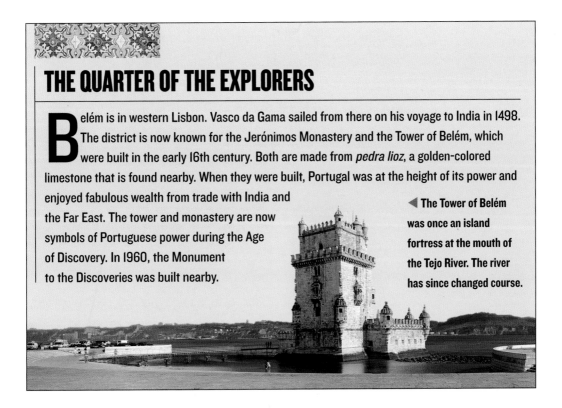

◄ The Tower of Belém was once an island fortress at the mouth of the Tejo River. The river has since changed course.

# DISASTER IN LISBON

On All Saints' Day—November 1—in 1755, the churches of Lisbon were full of people celebrating the country's good fortune. The city was growing rich on the gold that had just started coming from Brazil. Then the city was struck by one of the largest earthquakes ever recorded, demolishing churches, palaces, and houses. About 60,000 people died and 12,000 buildings were destroyed as the Tejo flooded the city.

Under the control of the Marquis of Pombal, the city was swiftly rebuilt with a new urban grid plan of avenues and squares. The new city center, named Baixa Pombalina (Pombal's lower city), was Europe's first planned city. The quake ended the fashion for complicated architecture. The new buildings

▲ During the earthquake, Lisbon was swamped by a tidal wave that surged up the Tejo River.

were in the simpler neoclassical style like other powerful European cities. Nevertheless the earthquake marked the end of Portugal's leading role in the world as Britain, France, and Spain took its place.

Through trade agreements between Portugal and Britain, the Brazilian gold ended up in London and was used to build factories, roads, and bridges and made Britain the most modern country in the world at the time. Products made in British factories were then shipped to Portugal in return for the gold.

The next king, José I, left the running of the country to his minister the Marquis of Pombal. Pombal was a good ruler, who realized that the country needed to modernize. After an earthquake destroyed Lisbon in 1755, he began a remarkable rebuilding program. Pombal also weakened the control of Portugal's noble families and of the Jesuits—a religious order that had a large say in the running of the country. However, Pombal's vision of a modern Portugal was never achieved. After King José I died, Pombal was removed from office, and the noble families and churches took control once again.

## Ruling From Abroad

In the early 1800s, the French under Emperor Napoleon Bonaparte invaded Portugal. In 1807 King João VI fled to Brazil with his government. For the next 14 years, the King of Portugal only ruled Brazil! João returned to Lisbon in 1821. (He left his son Pedro to run Brazil and one year later, Pedro made Brazil an independent country.) João VI arrived in Lisbon to find the country in turmoil as people fought over what type of government Portugal should have. The fighting continued for the rest of the century. In 1908 King Carlos I was assassinated. In 1910, his son, King

## THE LUSIADS

Luís Vaz de Camões is Portugal's national poet. He led an adventurous life during the 16th century, sailing to Morocco and then India. He wrote an epic poem called *Os Lusíadas* in 1572. The name comes from Lusitania, the Roman name for Portugal, and could be translated as *The Portuguese*. It tells the story of the voyages of Vasco da Gama and is still a symbol of Portuguese identity.

▲ Vasco da Gama presents a letter to the king of Calicut in western India as described in *Os Lusíadas*.

Manuel II gave up the throne, and Portugal became a republic.

# *Power Struggle*

The new republic did not bring peace. Between 1910 and 1926, Portugal had 44 governments, 20 coups d'état (military takeovers), and 12 presidents. The country became bankrupt. This period of chaos is now known as the First Republic.

In 1928 António de Oliveira Salazar became finance minister and achieved some economic stability. He went on to become prime minister in 1932. Salazar then became a dictator, but the stability his regime brought was welcomed by many Portuguese after the failures of the First Republic.

Portugal stayed neutral during World War II (1939–1945) and was a gateway for many refugees fleeing

the fighting in Europe. Salazar held on to power for several decades until his death in 1970.

## The Carnation Revolution

By this time Portugal had become an isolated country. It was fighting wars in its African colonies and its economy was poor. After the death of Salazar, the situation did not improve, and a group of army officers took over the country in a peaceful coup in 1974. However, the Portuguese people did not want to exchange one dictator for another, and they forced the new government to adopt democracy. The mass movement became known as the Carnation Revolution, because the rebels wore red carnations as their symbol. Portugal achieved its first real democratic government in 1976, and Portugal's remaining colonies in Africa, such as Mozambique and Angola, were given independence.

▲ A soldier shows his support for democracy by wearing a red carnation during the largely peaceful revolution of 1974.

## Back on the West Coast

Portugal joined what is now the European Union (EU) in 1986 and began to catch up with other European countries. In 1999 Portugal converted its currency to the euro like most EU countries. However, Portugal is still looking beyond Europe and maintains strong links with Brazil and other Portuguese-speaking countries.

# Saudade!

**P**ORTUGUESE HAS A WORD THAT cannot be translated into English. *Saudade* means a longing for something or someone that has gone or that is very far away. The word is used in many early Portuguese poems and came to express a national feeling during the Age of Discovery, when so many Portuguese left the country on long voyages, often never to return. Later, the meaning of saudade changed to represent the homesickness of the people living in the many Portuguese colonies around the world. Today saudade is used to describe the end of Portugal's "Golden Age," when Portugal was a leading power and the richest country in the world. The emotions of saudade are best expressed in a *fado*, a form of traditional Portuguese song.

◀ A Lisbon man sings a fado in a tavern in the city's ancient Alfama district. Anyone can sing if they want, accompanied by the bar's own lute players.

## At a Glance

# PLENTY OF SPACE

Portugal is not a crowded country, with an average of just 280 people per square mile (108 per square km). Between 1984 and 1994 the population even went down slightly, although it is rising again now. People are not spread evenly across the small country: Two-thirds of the population lives in the countryside, but the mountainous north is much less populated than the south. The most crowded areas are around the two largest cities, Lisbon (680,000 people) and Porto (350,000 people). The island of Madeira is also heavily populated.

| 1950 / 8.4 million | 1970 / 8.7 million |
|---|---|
| 19% urban / 81% rural | 30% urban / 70% rural |

| 1990 / 10.0 million | 2005 / 10.5 million |
|---|---|
| 47% urban / 53% rural | 56% urban / 44% rural |

## Common Portuguese Phrases

The Portuguese language became distinct from Castilian (Spanish) and the other languages spoken in the Iberian Peninsula during the period of Roman rule more than 2,000 years ago. Here are a few Portuguese words and phrases. Give them a try:

| | |
|---|---|
| How do you do? | Como está? |
| Hello (on the telephone) | Olá, Alô |
| Good morning | Bom dia |
| Good afternoon | Boa tarde |
| Good evening/Good night | Boa noite |
| Good-bye | Adeus |
| Please | Por favor |
| Thank you | Obrigado (said by a man) |
| | Obrigada (said by a woman) |
| Yes | Sim |
| No | No |
| My name is | Meu nome é |
| Sorry | Desculpe |

▼ Portugal is unusual for a European country: most of its people live in farming communities outside of cities.

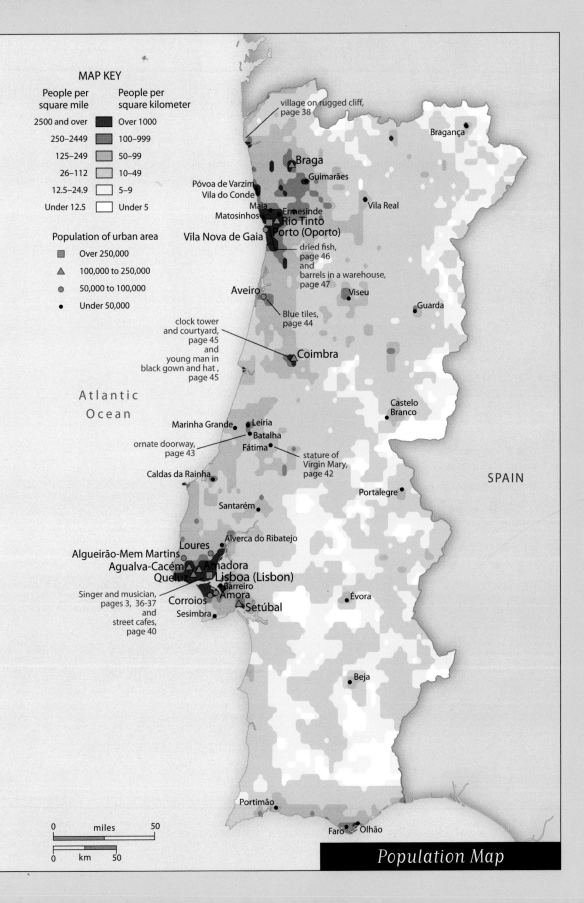

## MAP KEY

| People per square mile | People per square kilometer |
|---|---|
| 2500 and over | Over 1000 |
| 250–2449 | 100–999 |
| 125–249 | 50–99 |
| 26–112 | 10–49 |
| 12.5–24.9 | 5–9 |
| Under 12.5 | Under 5 |

Population of urban area

| | |
|---|---|
| ▢ | Over 250,000 |
| △ | 100,000 to 250,000 |
| ● | 50,000 to 100,000 |
| • | Under 50,000 |

village on rugged cliff, page 38

Bragança

Braga

Guimarães

Póvoa de Varzim
Vila do Conde

Vila Real

Maia
Matosinhos

Ermesinde
Rio Tinto
Porto (Oporto)

Vila Nova de Gaia

dried fish, page 46
and
barrels in a warehouse, page 47

Aveiro

Viseu

Guarda

Blue tiles, page 44

clock tower
and courtyard,
page 45
and
young man in
black gown and hat,
page 45

Coimbra

Atlantic
Ocean

Castelo
Branco

Marinha Grande

Leiria

Batalha

Fátima

ornate doorway,
page 43

stature of
Virgin Mary,
page 42

Caldas da Rainha

SPAIN

Portalegre

Santarém

Alverca do Ribatejo

Loures

Algueirão-Mem Martins

Agualva-Cacém

Amadora

Queluz

Lisboa (Lisbon)

Barreiro

Singer and musician,
pages 3, 36-37
and
street cafes,
page 40

Amora

Corroios

Sesimbra

Setúbal

Évora

Beja

Portimão

Faro    Olhão

miles

0    50

0    km    50

Population Map

# Staying the Same

In spite of its long history of exploration and distant colonies, Portugal has remained a homogenous place —its people all live in similar ways. Ninety percent of the population is of Portuguese origin, belonging to the same ethnic group that lived in the region during Roman times. The rest of the country is made up mainly of people from Brazil and a few hundred thousand people from the old colonies in Africa and Asia, such as Mozambique, Angola, and Macau.

# Home and Away

For the last century, Portugal has been a country of emigrants. People left Portugal for economic reasons.

Some went to find work in the more industrialized countries of northern Europe. Others went to seek their fortune in the colonies, especially Brazil, which was by now an independent country.

Following the revolution in the mid-1970s, Portugal granted independence to its African colonies. This process was done too hastily, and the new countries soon became unstable places—most began long civil wars.

Hundreds of thousands of Portuguese citizens living in Africa decided to come back to Portugal. These people were called *retornados*—the returnees. About 4.5 million Portuguese still live abroad, but in recent years more are returning as the country grows richer. The lure of jobs is also attracting workers from other European nations.

## Deep Faith

Nine out of ten Portuguese people are Roman Catholics. The rural north is more religious, with more people there attending

# NATIONAL HOLIDAYS

The most important holidays in Portugal are religious festivals. Each town has a patron saint and residents celebrate his or her feast day with a holiday each year. The main national holidays are the Christian feast days. There are some non-religious holidays: Freedom Day commemorates the Carnation Revolution in 1974. Portugal Day is on the date of the death of Camões, the national poet, who died in 1580. Republic Day remembers the founding of the republic in 1910, and the Restoration of Independence Day marks the end of the union with Spain in 1640.

▲ Colorful celebrations during a festival in Madeira

| JANUARY 1 | New Year's Day |
|---|---|
| FEBRUARY | Shrove Tuesday |
| MARCH/APRIL | Easter |
| APRIL 25 | Freedom Day |
| MAY 1 | Labour Day |
| MAY/JUNE | Corpus Christi |
| JUNE 10 | Portugal Day |
| AUGUST 15 | Feast of the Assumption |
| OCTOBER 5 | Republic Day |
| NOVEMBER 1 | All Saints' Day |
| DECEMBER 1 | Restoration of Independence Day |
| DECEMBER 8 | Feast of the Immaculate Conception |
| DECEMBER 25 | Christmas Day |

▲ Loaves of bread are paraded through the streets during a saint's day celebration on Pico Island in the Azores.

church than in the bustling southern region. Portugal is dotted with churches in prominent squares in every village and town or on hilltops. Saints' days and other religious festivals are very popular events. The whole village turns out. The celebrations begin with a

## THE SECRETS OF FÁTIMA

The town of Fátima in central Portugal has been an important pilgrimage site for Roman Catholics since three peasant children saw a vision of the Virgin Mary there in 1917. Only the children could see the vision, and only one girl could hear Mary speak. She passed on three secrets that many believe predicted later events of the 20th century. The vision is remembered by a candlelit procession on the 12th of every month from May to October. Hundreds of thousands of pilgrims visit the town during this time. In 1967, 1.5 million worshippers celebrated the 50th anniversary of the miracle.

▲ A small statue of the Virgin Mary is paraded through the streets of Fátima.

romaria—a religious procession—which is followed by a party with music, dancing, and a fun fair.

# Hammer Time!

Each town celebrates its own patron saint. These celebrations can take many forms. In June, the citizens of Porto celebrate the feast of Saint John in a very unusual way. People used to hit each other over the head with leeks as part of the fun in the city's streets! Today the flexible vegetables have been replaced with soft plastic hammers to prevent injuries.

There is a fireworks display above the Douro River and then people head to the beach, where they light fires and jump through the flames.

# Stylish Buildings

Having had such a long history, Portugal has a huge number of buildings built at different times in a range of architectural styles. Because the country was slow to modernize, there are many old buildings still standing to tell us their history. There are prehistoric burial mounds in the Peneda-Gerês national park. There are many ruins left from Roman times, including the

▲ The monastery at Batalha was begun in 1385 by João I, the first king in the House of Avis. It took 150 years to complete and is an excellent example of Portugal's Gothic architecture.

# A TALENT FOR TILES

For over 500 years, one of the most popular forms of Portuguese art has been painted and glazed tiles known as *azulejos*. The production technique was introduced to Portugal by the Moors, who used tiles to decorate mosques. The style was adopted by King Manuel I to decorate his palace in Sintra in the 1500s. The fashion for azulejos spread across Portugal, and the tiles appeared on both the insides and outsides of buildings. The characteristic blue and white tiles were most common in the 18th century, but today other colors are also used. Modern artists who have continued the tradition include Paula Rego and Maria Keil.

▲ The fronts of these houses have azulejos tiles showing scenes of the Portuguese way of life.

remains of an ancient city at Conimbriga. The great wars between the Moorish and Christian armies have left their mark, too, with the massive castles built at the time still seen on many hilltops.

The most distinctively Portuguese type of architecture is the Manueline style with its seafaring symbols. These buildings were constructed to celebrate achievements during the Age of Discovery in the 16th century. Many Manueline-style buildings, such as the Jerónimos Monastery, Tower of Belém, and part of the Monastery of Batalha are being preserved for the future by the United Nations.

The gold that came from Brazil during the 18th century was used to pay for—and decorate—many churches and palaces. One famous church in Portugal is the Church of Bom Jesus do Monte outside Braga. It can be seen for miles around on a hilltop and is reached by a long flight of steps.

## Teaching Children

Traditionally, large families are at the center of Portuguese society. Grandparents, aunts, and uncles all help to bring up children. Family members live close together. In the countryside, when someone gets married or has a child, they do not move away into their own house—their parents just add more rooms or an apartment to the family home.

▲ A college student in a sash at his graduation. The patches on the sash show his memories of his time at school.

▼ The University of Coimbra is the oldest college in Portugal. It was founded in 1290 and is still one of the top schools in Europe.

## SALTY STORIES

One of the most popular Portuguese foods is *bacalhau* or salted cod. Cod has played a big part in Portuguese history. It was one of the things Portuguese sailors were looking for as they explored the ocean. Portugal's fishermen were catching cod on the Grand Banks near Canada probably before the voyage of Columbus. They preserved their catch with salt because refrigeration had not been invented. Salted cod feels like cardboard and needs to be soaked in water for hours before it is ready to cook. It is said that there are more than 365 ways to cook bacalhau—one for every day of the year.

▲ A large salted cod is wrapped in a shop. Many Portuguese families eat cod for their Christmas meal.

▼ The Portuguese eat a lot of seafood, including octopus. Chunks are added to stews and salads, and it is also eaten whole.

Children go to kindergarten from the age of 3 to the age of 6 and then grade school until age 15. High school education is available but is not required. However, many people choose to go on to college. The competition for university placement is intense.

Student life in Portugal is fun. They may live in housing called *repúblicas*, where residents follow old rituals. For example, they each burn a ribbon to mark the end of their studies.

## World Food

Portuguese food is similar to that of other southern European countries. Fresh vegetables, fish, and meat are cooked in olive oil and garlic. Other flavorings and spices from Portugal's former colonies in Asia, Africa, and South America, are also used including cloves, cinnamon, vanilla, and saffron.

Soups are very common. The most famous are *canja de galinha*—chicken soup with rice—and *caldo verde*—a dish of potatoes and cabbage.

Portuguese people eat freshly caught fish and shellfish several times a week. Pork is a favorite meat and is cooked in a variety of ways. In the Alentejo region it is often served with clams. Portuguese desserts and sweet snacks are patisseries—thin pastries and pies—filled with fruits, custards, and cream.

Portugal is the seventh-largest producer of wine in the world. The most famous is the *vinho do Porto*. Also known as simply Port, these sweet wines are produced in the Douro River Valley.

## THE QUEEN OF FATE

Amália Rodrigues was the most famous singer of fado, Portugal's national music. The fado style of chanting is like the songs performed by traveling singers in the Middle Ages. At that time the songs were a way of spreading news and remembering important events. In the 19th century, similar songs, often about life at sea or the lives of the poor, became known as fados. Fado means "fate." Known simply by her first name, Amália had a 40-year career during which she made the fado style world famous. Thousands of people gathered for her funeral in 1999 (pictured), and her loss was so great, the government declared three days of national mourning.

▼ A warehouse in Porto is filled with barrels of Port wine. Only wine from northern Portugal can use that name.

# New for Old

**P**ORTUGAL'S ENTRY INTO THE European Union in 1986 was an important moment. After many decades of being isolated from the world by a dictator, better links with its neighbors in Europe transformed Portugal into a very modern country. Several events have helped highlight Portugal's great changes. Lisbon was elected European Capital of Culture in 1994, and Portugal's artists began to be recognized around the world. José Saramago was the first Portuguese writer to receive the Nobel Prize for Literature in 1998. The biggest boost came with the Expo '98 international trade fair held in Lisbon. This marked the 500th year since Vasco da Gama's voyage. It was celebrated with a new bridge over the Tejo—still the longest bridge in Europe at over 11 miles (17 km).

◀ Lisbon's Vasco da Gama Tower was built for the Expo '98 event. The curved steel structure is meant to represent the sails that powered da Gama's small ships to India.

# POLITICAL SYSTEM

▼ The Portuguese parliament applauds as the Lisbon Treaty—an EU-wide agreement made in the city—becomes law in 2008.

After the many political and economic problems of the 20th century, Portugal is now a properly functioning democracy. Since 2000, power has swung between different political parties a few times, but the country has continued to prosper. The main political parties are the Socialist Party (PS), the Social Democratic Party (PSD), and the Portuguese Communist-Green Alliance (CDU).

Portugal is divided into 18 districts. The districts are further divided into 305 smaller *concelhos*, and these are subdivided into 4,200 *freguesias*. The islands of the Azores and Madeira have their own regional governments.

## Trading Partners

Portugal's main trading partners are its fellow members of the European Union. Its large neighbor, Spain, is by far its major partner. Until the 1970s, Portugal's economy was based on trade with its African colonies. This business declined greatly after the colonies became independent, but trade with Brazil, another former colony, has increased in recent years. Portugal exports cars, textiles, paper, wine, and cork. It imports food and fuel.

| Country | Percentage Portugal exports |
| --- | --- |
| Spain | 27.4% |
| Germany | 13.1% |
| France | 12.4% |
| United Kingdom | 7.1% |
| All others combined | 40.0% |

| Country | Percentage Portugal imports |
| --- | --- |
| Spain | 30.5% |
| Germany | 13.8% |
| France | 8.4% |
| Italy | 5.8% |
| All others combined | 41.5% |

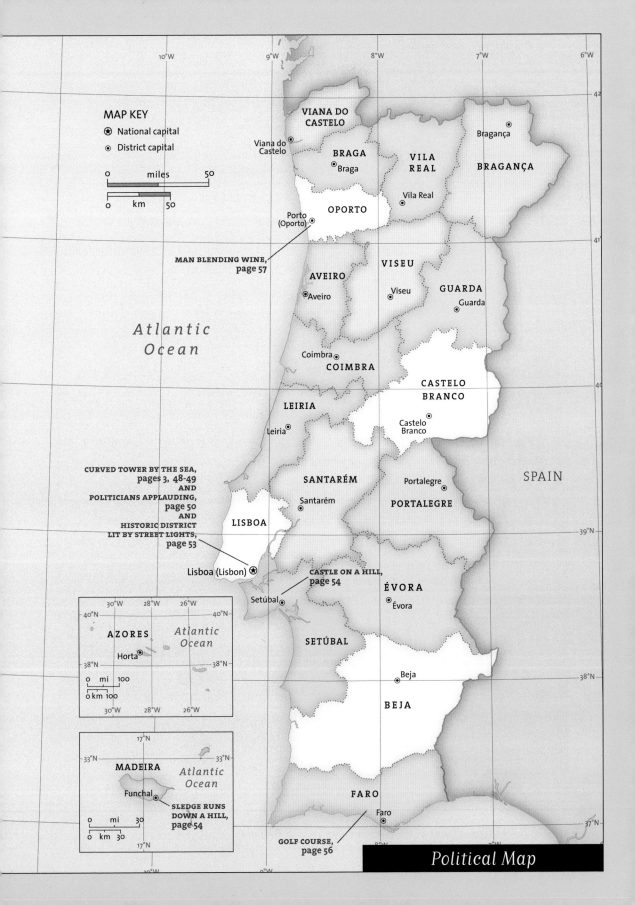

MAP KEY

⊛ National capital

⊙ District capital

miles 50

km 50

**VIANA DO CASTELO**

Viana do Castelo ⊙

**BRAGA**

Braga ⊙

**VILA REAL**

Vila Real ⊙

Bragança ⊙

**BRAGANÇA**

**OPORTO**

Porto (Oporto) ⊙

MAN BLENDING WINE, page 57

**VISEU**

Viseu ⊙

**GUARDA**

Guarda ⊙

**AVEIRO**

Aveiro ⊙

*Atlantic Ocean*

Coimbra ⊙

**COIMBRA**

**CASTELO BRANCO**

Castelo Branco ⊙

**LEIRIA**

Leiria ⊙

CURVED TOWER BY THE SEA, pages 3, 48-49 AND POLITICIANS APPLAUDING, page 50 AND HISTORIC DISTRICT LIT BY STREET LIGHTS, page 53

**SANTARÉM**

Santarém ⊙

Portalegre ⊙

**PORTALEGRE**

SPAIN

**LISBOA**

Lisboa (Lisbon) ⊛

CASTLE ON A HILL, page 54

**ÉVORA**

Évora ⊙

Setúbal ⊙

**SETÚBAL**

Beja ⊙

**BEJA**

Horta ⊙

**AZORES**

*Atlantic Ocean*

mi 100

km 100

**FARO**

Faro ⊙

**MADEIRA**

*Atlantic Ocean*

Funchal ⊙

SLEDGE RUNS DOWN A HILL, page 54

mi 30

km 30

GOLF COURSE, page 56

Political Map

# Democratic Process

With the revolution of 1974, dictatorship ended in Portugal and democracy began. There was a new constitution in 1976, but the early years of democracy were just as chaotic as the First Republic. There were 12 different governments in 5 years. It was not until the 1980s that the political situation started to settle with the election of President Mário Soares and Prime Minister Aníbal Cavaco Silva. Parliament revised the constitution in 1982 and stayed in power until 1995, bringing a much-needed period of political stability.

# HOW GOVERNMENT WORKS

Portugal is a democratic republic with a mixed form of government run by both an elected president and a parliament. The president is the head of state but the prime minister is the head of the government. The prime minister is the leader of the largest party in parliament and governs with the help of the Council of Ministers. Ministers are appointed by the president but following recommendations from the prime minister. The president is elected by all adult citizens. He or she serves for a five-year period and can be re-elected only once. There are 230 seats in the parliament—the Assembleia da República. Members are elected for a four-year term. The president has limited powers but calls elections when the government loses the support of the parliament and can also propose changes to the constitution. The country's main court is the Supreme Court of Justice. Its judges are appointed by the parliament.

| GOVERNMENT | | |
| --- | --- | --- |
| EXECUTIVE | LEGISLATIVE | JUDICIARY |
| PRESIDENT | PARLIAMENT (230 MEMBERS) | SUPREME COURT OF JUSTICE |
| GOVERNMENT | GOVERNMENT | CONSTITUTIONAL COURT |

Portugal joined what is now the European Union (EU) in 1986. Since then the country has modernized very rapidly thanks to the money given to it by richer, more-developed countries. In 1999, Portugal adopted the euro—a new currency being used by many countries in Europe.

## A Welcome Legacy

Being an isolated, old-fashioned place for so many years was not all bad for Portugal. While its neighbors built huge cities and ugly industrial areas too quickly and without proper planning, Portuguese cities have kept much of their historic character and old buildings. The natural environment is also well preserved; there is no serious pollution in Portugal.

Since the 1980s, the large gap in living standards between Portugal and the rest of western Europe has been cut in half. Portuguese people are still quite poor compared to those of other countries, but the difference is now much smaller than it was.

## You're Welcome!

*Bem receber* means "good hospitality" in Portuguese. Hospitality, together with a mild climate,

▲ Mário Soares became Portugal's president in 1980 and dominated the country until 1996.

▼ Apart from the street lights, Lisbon has not changed that much since the late 18th century.

long coastline, and a wide range of landscapes and historical sites, has made Portugal into a major tourist destination.

Tourism has contributed a lot to the country's economy. It employs nearly 8 percent of the work force and generates 6.5 percent of the country's wealth each year. Portugal is one of the world's most visited countries. In 2006, Portugal received 13 million foreign visitors, mostly from northern European countries such as Britain, Germany, and Scandinavia.

The tourism industry has changed many areas, in particular the Algarve. The government is trying to develop tourism without destroying the character of the country that attracts the tourists in the first place.

▲ Tourists are pushed down a steep street in Funchal, Madeira, in a sled steered by two *carreiros*. The sled's runners are coated with wax to help them slide.

## CAN I STAY IN THE DUNGEON?

As part of its drive to encourage tourism, the Portuguese government has converted more than 40 of the country's historic buildings—castles, palaces, monasteries, and manor houses—into luxury hotels known as *pousadas*. Guests can stroll through the courtyards or along the ramparts and enjoy staying in rooms that 16th-century monks and warriors have used. Despite being based in old buildings, the pousadas offer maximum luxury with good service and fine food.

▲ Palmela Castle was a Moorish castle in the 12th century but is now a luxury hotel.

# Lusofonia

Although Portugal has worked hard to make stronger links with the rest of Europe, it has also strengthened ties with its former colonies on other continents. Together these countries form Lusofonia—the areas of the world where people speak Portuguese. It is estimated that about 200 million people speak the language, mostly in Brazil. In 1996 the loose group of countries was made into a proper organization: The Community of Portuguese-Speaking Countries.

# Wine and Cork

Two of Portugal's main exports are wine and the corks used to seal the bottles. The country produces some unique styles of wine. The most famous are Port and

▲ Athletes compete at the first Lusofonia Games in Macau in 2006. The competitors come from all corners of the world—Portugal, Sri Lanka, Brazil, and Mozambique: countries that were once ruled from Lisbon.

Madeira. Port is very sweet and fruity, and it keeps its flavor for a long time. Madeira is often used in cooking, especially for meat dishes and cakes.

Port was the first wine to have its place of production recognized and protected by law in 1756. It is produced in the Douro Valley, in the mountainous north of the country. The name comes from the city of Porto. Most of the Port wine businesses, known as lodges, were started by British merchants in the 18th century. At that time Britain was at war with France and could not buy wine from their enemy. So the British merchants bought it from Portugal instead.

Wine producers were looking for ways to sell their product in bottles instead of barrels. However, bottle tops of the time let in air and made the Port stale. Luckily, Portugal had a ready supply of cork, which

## SPORTUGAL

Tourism has become a very important part of the Portuguese economy, and in the south of the country, many tourists come for the sports. The Portuguese climate and the availability of land have made the Algarve one of the great golfing destinations in the world. There are 29 courses along the 100 miles (160 km) of the Algarve coast. Visitors play a million rounds of golf on the Algarve each year. Other popular activities are tennis, windsurfing, and fishing.

▲ Many Algarve golf courses are on the coast with lots of obstacles made by beaches and dunes.

# INDUSTRY

Portugal is the least industrialized country in western Europe. The traditional businesses of agriculture, fishing, and forestry are still the largest industries in Portugal. New industries, such as manufacturing cars, have been established since the country joined the EU. However, Portugal still imports more than it exports, which is a problem for the economy. Today a third of the population works in manufacturing. The major industrial centers are Lisbon, Porto, Setúbal, and Sines. Most industries are still run as small businesses. The Alentejo is the main mining area, producing copper, limestone, and marble.

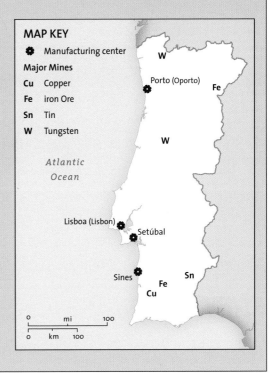

MAP KEY
- ⚙ Manufacturing center

Major Mines
- Cu  Copper
- Fe  iron Ore
- Sn  Tin
- W  Tungsten

Atlantic Ocean

Porto (Oporto) · W · Fe

W

Lisboa (Lisbon) · Setúbal

Sines · Fe · Sn

Cu

mi 100

km 100

could make airtight stoppers. Wine stored in corked bottles stays fresh for decades. Cork is still used to seal wine bottles, but it is expensive. Modern bottles have screw tops, reducing the demand for Portugal's cork.

▼ **An expert blends Port wine to make the best-tasting product at a winery in Porto.**

## On the Upswing

As it was 500 years ago, Portugal is again an important link between Europe and the rest of the world. In the last 20 years, Portugal has emerged as a modern, businesslike country. The Portuguese are working to fulfill a hope sung in their national anthem: "Rise again today the splendor of Portugal."

# Add a Little Extra to Your Country Report!

If you are assigned to write a report about Portugal, you'll want to include basic information about the country, of course. The Fast Facts chart on page 8 will give you a good start. The rest of the book will give you the details you need to create a full and up-to-date paper or PowerPoint presentation. But what can you do to make your report more fun than anyone else's? If you use your imagination and dig a bit deeper into some of the topics introduced in this book, you're sure to come up with information that will make your report unique!

## >Flag

Perhaps you could explain the history of Portugal's flag, and the meanings of its colors and symbols. Go to **www.crwflags.com/fotw/flags** for more information.

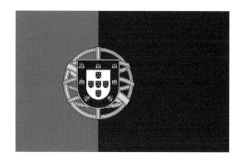

## >National Anthem

How about downloading Portugal's national anthem and playing it for your class? At **www.nationalanthems.info** you'll find what you need, including the words to the anthem, plus sheet music for it. Simply pick "P" and then "Portugal" from the list on the left of the screen, and you're on your way.

## >Time Difference

If you want to understand the time difference between Portugal and where you are, this Web site can help: **www.worldtimeserver.com**. First, select "Current Times" at the top of the page. Then pick "Portugal" from the list at the right. If you called someone in Portugal right now, would you wake them up from their sleep?

## >*Currency*

Another Web site will convert your money into euros, the currency used in Portugal. You'll want to know how much money to bring if you're ever lucky enough to travel to Portugal: **www.xe.com/ucc.**

## >*Weather*

Why not check the current weather in Portugal? It's easy—go to **www.weather.com** to find out if it's sunny or cloudy, warm or cold in Portugal right now! Pick "World" from the headings at the top of the page. Then search for any Portuguese city. Click on "Current Weather." You can get Sunrise/Sunset information, too. Scroll down the page for the 36-Hour Forecast and a satellite weather map. Compare your weather to the weather in the Portuguese city you chose. Is this a good season, weather-wise, for a person to travel to Portugal?

## >*Miscellaneous*

Still want more information? Simply go to National Geographic's World Atlas for Young Explorers at **http://www.nationalgeographic.com/ kids-world-atlas.** It will help you find maps, photos, music, games, and other features that you can use to jazz up your report.

# Glossary

**Annexed** when a territory becomes part of another country. For example, Portugal was annexed by Spain between 1580 and 1640.

**Architecture** the style used to construct and decorate a building.

**Cabinet** a group of politicians who run a country. Each member of the cabinet is called a minister and is in charge of a particular part of the government.

**Civil war** when two or more groups living in the same country fight each other for control of all or part of the territory.

**Climate** the average weather of a certain place at different times of year.

**Colony** a region that is ruled by a nation located somewhere else in the world. Settlers from that distant country take over the land from the region's original inhabitants.

**Culture** a collection of beliefs, traditions, and styles that belongs to people living in a certain part of the world.

**Democracy** a country that is ruled by a government chosen by all its people through elections.

**Dictator** a leader who has complete control over a country and does not have to be elected or re-elected to office regularly. Dictators are often cruel and corrupt.

**Economy** the system by which a country creates wealth through making and trading products.

**Endangered** an animal or plant that is at risk of dying out.

**Ethnic group** a section of a country's population with members that share a common ancestry or background.

**Exported** transported and sold outside the country of origin.

**Fertile** capable of supporting new life.

**Glazed** when pottery is covered in a glassy coating to make it waterproof.

**Imported** brought into the country from abroad.

**Independent** self-governing.

**Maritime** related to the ocean.

**Middle Ages** a period of history from A.D. 500 to 1500.

**Monarchy** a system of government that is headed by a king or queen.

**Patron saint** a country's or town's main saint.

**Pilgrimage** a journey made to visit a religious shrine.

**Province** a region within a country that has some degree of control over its own affairs.

**Republic** a country that is headed by an elected president.

**Revolution** a rapid, often violent change of government when a large number of the country's people demand change.

**Roman Catholic** a Christian who follows the branch of the religion based in Rome, Italy.

**Species** a type of organism; animals or plants in the same species look similar and can only breed successfully among themselves.

# Bibliography

Rose, Elizabeth. *A Primary Source Guide to Portugal.* New York, NY: PowerKids Press, 2004.

Italia, Bob. *Portugal.* Edina, MN: Abdo, 2002.

http://www.portugal.gov.pt/ Portal/EN/Portugal/ (English-language Web site provided by the government of Portugal with general information about the country)

http://www.portugal.org/ index.shtml (official government Web site)

# Further Information

## NATIONAL GEOGRAPHIC Articles

Graves, William. "After an Empire … Portugal." NATIONAL GEOGRAPHIC (December 1980): 804–831.

## Web sites to explore

More fast facts about Portugal, from the CIA (Central Intelligence Agency): https://www.cia.gov/library/ publications/the-world-fact-book/geos/po.html

Find out more about the voyage of Vasco da Gama, Portugal's most celebrated explorer, at this Web site complete with animated maps: http://www.ucalgary.ca/ applied_history/tutor/ eurvoya/vasco.html

See how Portugal expanded and then lost its empire using this interactive time line: http://www.timelines.info/ history/empires_and_ civilizations/portuguese_ empire/

Take a look at the extraordinary beauty of the Azores, Portugal's remote, tropical islands, at http://www.azoresweb.com/ introduction_azores.html

Portugal has several national parks and nature reserves. See pictures and find out more about them at this Web site: http://www.manorhouses.com/ parks/

Portuguese fishers once used dogs to herd fish in shallow water into their nets. The breed they use is called the Portuguese water dog, which is similar to the poodle. Find out what they look like and

how they were bred at: http://www.dogbreedinfo.com/ portuguesewaterdog.htm

## See, hear

There are many ways to get a taste of life in Portugal, such as movies and music. You might be able to locate these:

*The Portugal News*
An English-language newspaper produced in Portugal and available online at: http://the-news.net/

*Get Real Weekly*
A magazine in English produced each week in Faro, Portugal. Browse through each edition online at: http://www. getrealweekly.com

# Index

# Credits

## Picture Credits

Front Cover – Spine: javarman/Shutterstock; Top: Thomas Peter Widmann/Alamy; Low Far Left: Fernando Bengoechea/Beateworks/Corbis; Low Left: George McCarthy /Corbis; Low Right: James L. Stanfield/NGIC; Low Far Right: Abraham Norritz/NGIC.

Interior – Corbis: Tony Arruza: 23 up; Fernando Bengoechea/Beateworks: 46 lo; Bettmann: 32, 33, 34 up; Tibor Bognar: 45 lo; Henri Bureau/Sygma: 35; Jan Butchofsky-Houser: 45 up; Ashley Cooper: 26 up; Mario Cruz: 50; Jose Fuste Raga: 2 left, 6-7; Chinch Gryniewicz/Ecoscene: 2 right, 16-17; Hemis: 3 right, 48-49; Dave G. Houser: 40; Ray Juno: 11 lo, 41; Paulo Novais/epa: 42 lo; Fred de Noyelle/Godong: 31 up; Charles O' Rear: 5, 20 up, 28 lo, 47 lo, 54 lo; Michael Philippot/Sygma: 53 up; Puku/ Grand Tour: 54 up; Philippe Renault/Hemis: 56; Reuters: 47 up; Jose Manuel Ribeiro/Reuters: 46 up; Isabelle Vayron/Sygma: 3 left, 36-37; Getty Images: Ted Aljibe/AFP: 55; NGIC: Michael Fay: 15 up; Stephanie Maze: 21 up, 57 lo; O. Louis Mazzatena: 42 up; Flip Nicklin/Minden Pictures: 18 lo; Panoramic Stock Images: 14 up, 31 lo, 44: Robert Sisson: 30; Brian J. Skerry: 22 lo; Tino Soriano: 34 lo, 53 lo; James L. Stanfield: 10 lo, 12 up, 29, 43; Medford Taylor: 15 lo, 38 lo; Volkmar K. Wentzel: TP, 2-3, 12 lo, 13 right, 24-25; NPL: Roger Powell: 23 lo; Jose B. Ruiz: 20 lo; Shutterstock: Peter Dankov: 59

For information about special discounts for bulk purchases, contact National Geographic Special Sales: ngspecsales@ngs.org

For more information, please call 1-800-NGS-LINE (647-5463) or write to the following address:

NATIONAL GEOGRAPHIC SOCIETY
1145 17th Street N.W.
Washington, D.C. 20036-4688 U.S.A.

Visit us online at www.nationalgeographic.com/books

Library of Congress Cataloging-in-Publication Data available on request
ISBN: 978-1-4263-0390-6

Printed in the United States of America

Series design by Jim Hiscott.
The body text is set in Avenir; Knockout.
The display text is set in Matrix Script.

Front Cover—Top: A cable car ascends a steep street in Lisbon; Low Far Left: Monument to the Discoveries, Lisbon; Low Left: Octopus and peas; Low Right: A traditional painted home in the Algarve; Low Far Right: Blotched genet.

Page 1—Fishers guide their boat through heavy surf to the beach at Nazare.

## Produced through the worldwide resources of the National Geographic Society

John M. Fahey, Jr., *President and Chief Executive Officer*; Gilbert M. Grosvenor, *Chairman of the Board*; Tim T. Kelly, *President, Global Media Group*; John Q. Griffin, *President, Publishing*; Nina D. Hoffman, *Executive Vice President, President of Book Publishing Group*

## National Geographic Staff for this Book

Nancy Laties Feresten, *Vice President, Editor-in-Chief of Children's Books*
Bea Jackson, *Director of Design and Illustration*
Jim Hiscott, *Art Director*
Virginia Koeth, *Project Editor*
Lori Epstein, *Illustrations Editor*
Stacy Gold, Nadia Hughes, *Illustrations Research Editors*
R. Gary Colbert, *Production Director*
Lewis R. Bassford, *Production Manager*
Nicole Elliott, *Manufacturing Manager*
Maps, *Mapping Specialists, Ltd.*

## Brown Reference Group plc. Staff for this Book

*Volume Editor:* Tom Jackson
*Designer:* Dave Allen
*Picture Manager:* Sophie Mortimer
*Maps:* Martin Darlison
*Artwork:* Darren Awuah
*Index:* Kay Ollerenshaw
*Senior Managing Editor:* Tim Cooke
*Children's Publisher:* Anne O'Daly
*Editorial Director:* Lindsey Lowe

## About the Author

ZILAH DECKKER was born in Brazil and educated in Brazil and the United Kingdom, where she received a PhD in architectural history. She has visited Portugal many times, as a result of its close historical connection with the country of her birth.

## About the Consultants

TIMOTHY J. COATES is a professor of Iberian and Latin American history at the College of Charleston (South Carolina). His research and publications have been on the early modern Portuguese empire. He published *Convicts and Orphans* in 2001 and more recently co-authored a work in Portuguese on Castro Marim and internal exile in Portugal. He has taught and researched in Portugal for more than four years. In 2001, the president of Portugal decorated him with the medal of Commander of the Order of Saint James.

ANA FRANCISCA DE AZEVEDO is professor of cultural geography at the University of Minho, Portugal, where she teaches human geography, cultural geography, and the theory of geography. Her research focuses on cultural representations of space, place, and landscape, and the relations between geography, art, and visual culture. She is author of the book *A Ideia de Paisagem* (2008), along with other books and scientific publications. She did research on environmental and health education with the Danish Research Academy, and studied much of her PhD at University College, London, in the field of geography and cinema.